THIS COLORING BOOK BELONGS TO:

____

black
and
proud

THIS PAGE IS LEFT INTENTIONALLY BLANK TO
AVOID BLEED THROUGH

BLACK
COLOUR
IS NOT A
CRIME

THIS PAGE IS LEFT INTENTIONALLY BLANK TO
AVOID BLEED THROUGH

BLACK IS
BEAUTIFUL
MAGICAL
CULTURE
TALENT
family

Born
to be
Queen

THIS PAGE IS LEFT INTENTIONALLY BLANK TO AVOID BLEED THROUGH

STRONG
BEAUTY
SMART
POWERFUL
QUEEN

THIS PAGE IS LEFT INTENTIONALLY BLANK TO
AVOID BLEED THROUGH

All
Black
Women are
Queens

THIS PAGE IS LEFT INTENTIONALLY BLANK TO
AVOID BLEED THROUGH

Beautiful
Boss
Black

THIS PAGE IS LEFT INTENTIONALLY BLANK TO
AVOID BLEED THROUGH

Being
Black
is a
BLESSING

Black
Loud
and
Proud

THIS PAGE IS LEFT INTENTIONALLY BLANK TO AVOID BLEED THROUGH

Black
Queens
with
plump lips

THIS PAGE IS LEFT INTENTIONALLY BLANK TO
AVOID BLEED THROUGH

BLACKNIFICENT
Deity

THIS PAGE IS LEFT INTENTIONALLY BLANK TO
AVOID BLEED THROUGH

Brown
sugar
Beauty

THIS PAGE IS LEFT INTENTIONALLY BLANK TO
AVOID BLEED THROUGH

Chocolate
dipped
Beauty

Cocoa powder
Honey
dripping
GOLD

Envy
worthy
shades of
Melanin
Beauty

THIS PAGE IS LEFT INTENTIONALLY BLANK TO
AVOID BLEED THROUGH

I DON'T
apologize
FOR BEING
Black

Let these
curls do the
talking

Lips
honey
Sweeter
than

Mama told ME
to carry my
Heritage with
Pride

Melanin
Infused
Beauty

my Life may not be Perfect, but my Curls are

THIS PAGE IS LEFT INTENTIONALLY BLANK TO
AVOID BLEED THROUGH

Royalty
is in my
DNA

THIS PAGE IS LEFT INTENTIONALLY BLANK TO AVOID BLEED THROUGH

Royalty
is in my
& Heri
tage

THIS PAGE IS LEFT INTENTIONALLY BLANK TO AVOID BLEED THROUGH

Smart
Beautiful
Amazing
Brave
Kind

THIS PAGE IS LEFT INTENTIONALLY BLANK TO AVOID BLEED THROUGH

THICK
Beautiful
BLACK

THIS PAGE IS LEFT INTENTIONALLY BLANK TO AVOID BLEED THROUGH

This
Black Beauty
is a Queen

Black Women Are
DOPE

CROWN could be fixed
but the CHARACTER can't never be solved
the beauty always
comes from
Melanin's
HEART

I DON'T
apologize
FOR BEING
Black

THIS PAGE IS LEFT INTENTIONALLY BLANK TO
AVOID BLEED THROUGH

THICK
Beautiful
BLACK

THIS PAGE IS LEFT INTENTIONALLY BLANK TO
AVOID BLEED THROUGH

HER SOUL IS fierce
HER HEART IS brave
HER MIND IS strong

THIS PAGE IS LEFT INTENTIONALLY BLANK TO
AVOID BLEED THROUGH

BEAUTIFUL
black

THIS PAGE IS LEFT INTENTIONALLY BLANK TO
AVOID BLEED THROUGH

MADE WITH
MELANIN
ALWAYS POPPIN'

SAY IT LOUD
I'M
black
AND
proud

THIS PAGE IS LEFT INTENTIONALLY BLANK TO
AVOID BLEED THROUGH

MELANIN
QUEEN

beauty
is my
Business

THIS PAGE IS LEFT INTENTIONALLY BLANK TO
AVOID BLEED THROUGH

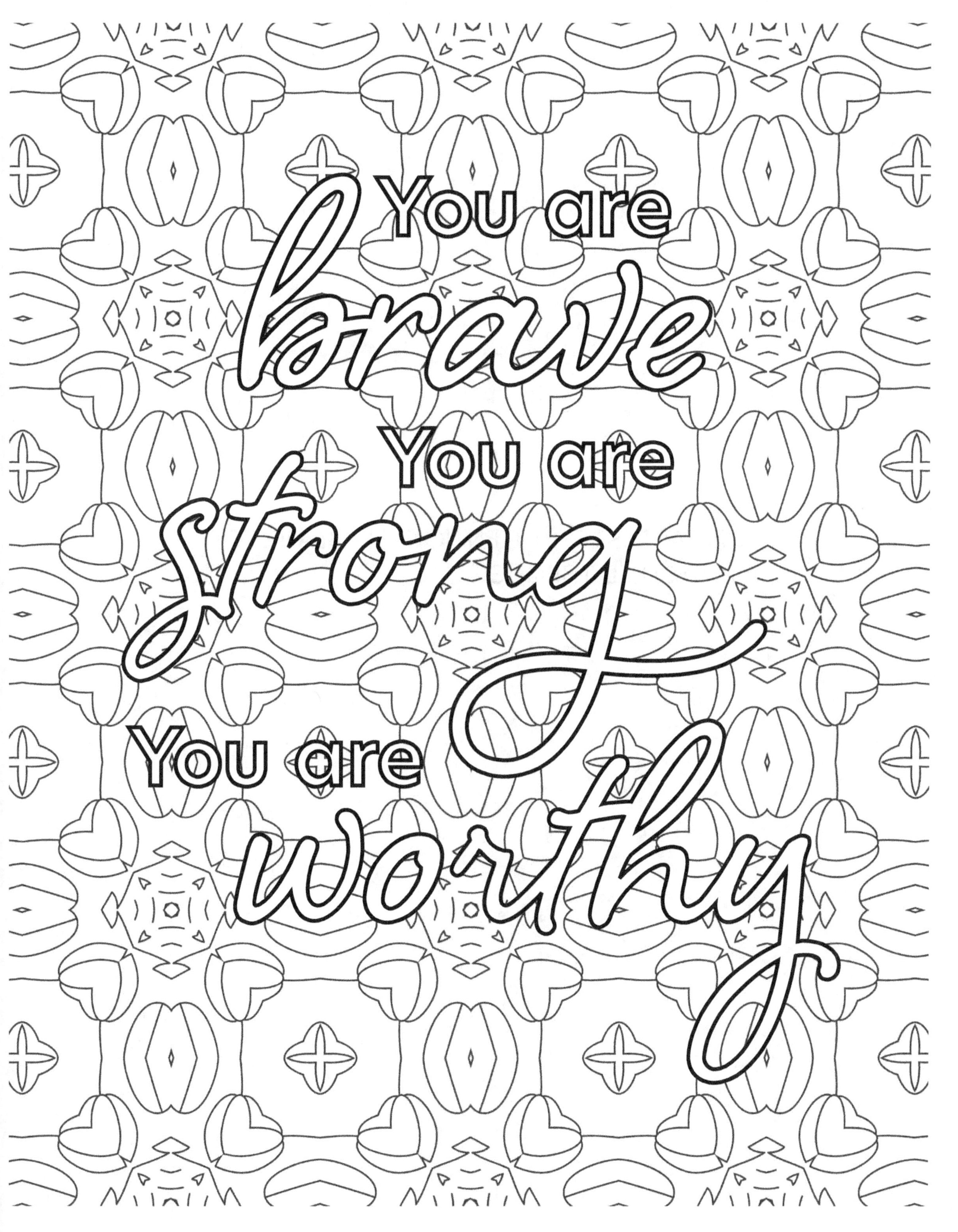

You are
brave
You are
strong
You are
worthy

darling, you are a work of art

THIS PAGE IS LEFT INTENTIONALLY BLANK TO
AVOID BLEED THROUGH

BEHIND EVERY
successful
WOMAN IS
herself

THIS PAGE IS LEFT INTENTIONALLY BLANK TO AVOID BLEED THROUGH

confident
WOMEN
empower
WOMEN

THIS PAGE IS LEFT INTENTIONALLY BLANK TO
AVOID BLEED THROUGH

GIRL, YOU
have no
IDEA HOW
strong
YOU ARE

THIS PAGE IS LEFT INTENTIONALLY BLANK TO
AVOID BLEED THROUGH

I SURVIVED
because the
FIRE INSIDE ME
burned
BRIGHTER

THIS PAGE IS LEFT INTENTIONALLY BLANK TO
AVOID BLEED THROUGH

NOT FRAGILE
like a flower
FRAGILE LIKE
a bomb

THIS PAGE IS LEFT INTENTIONALLY BLANK TO
AVOID BLEED THROUGH

I AM A BLACK QUEEN.
BEAUTIFUL AND BLACK.

THIS PAGE IS LEFT INTENTIONALLY BLANK TO
AVOID BLEED THROUGH

www.ingramcontent.com/pod-product-compliance
Lightning Source LLC
Chambersburg PA
CBHW081953260726
48657CB00009BA/2739